KED WONDERFUL

TOP 10:

HORRORS

By Virginia Loh-Hagan

45th Parallel Press

Published in the United States of America by Cherry Lake Publishing
Ann Arbor, Michigan
www.cherrylakepublishing.com

Content Adviser: Stephen Ditchkoff, Professor of Wildlife Ecology and Management, Auburn University, Alabama
Reading Adviser: Marla Conn MS, Ed., Literacy specialist, Read-Ability, Inc.
Book Designer: Melinda Millward

Photo Credits: ©Seread/Dreamstime.com, cover, 1, 14; ©Mgkuijpers/Dreamstime.com, 5; ©Bildagentur Zoonar GmbH/Shutterstock.com, 6; ©GUIDO BISSATTINI/Shutterstock.com, 6; ©kochanowski/Shutterstock.com, 6; ©Tom Tietz/Shutterstock.com, 7; ©Andyworks/iStockphoto, 8; ©Mikelane45/Dreamstime.com, 10; ©reptiles4all/Shutterstock.com, 10; ©Rudmer Zwerver/Shutterstock.com, 10; ©karlbarrett/iStockphoto, 11; ©Mik122/CanStock, 12; ©risteski goce/Shutterstock.com, 12; ©Flirt/Alamy Stock Photo, 13; ©Richard Seeley/Shutterstock.com, 14; ©Comstock Images/Thinkstock, 14; ©bikeriderlondon/Shutterstock.com, 15; ©tswinner/iStockphoto, 16; ©nitrogenic.com/Shutterstock.com, 16; ©Pieter De Pauw/iStockphoto, 16; ©vladoskan/Thinkstock, 17; ©Vibe Images/Shutterstock.com, 18; ©Oxford Scientific/ Getty Images, 20; ©Thomas Quine/http://www.flickr.com/CC-BY-2.0, 20; ©Michael Lynch/Shutterstock.com, 21; ©Marian Cernansky/Shutterstock.com, 22; ©Sebastian Janicki/Shutterstock.com, 22; ©Vinokurov Kirill/Shutterstock.com, 22; ©davemhuntphotography/Shutterstock.com, 23; ©Andrey Davidenko/Dreamstime.com, 24; ©StudioSmart/Shutterstock.com, 24; ©Alex_187/Shutterstock.com, 24; ©Lena Ason/Alamy Stock Photo, 25; ©TIKEPHOTO/Shutterstock.com, 26; ©Steve Byland/Dreamstime.com, 26; ©Audrey Snider-Bell/Shutterstock.com, 26; ©Neil Harrison/Dreamstime.com, 27; ©Matt Jeppson/Shutterstock.com, 28; ©Heiko Kiera/Shutterstock.com, 29; ©Sciepro/Getty Images, 30; ©toeytoey/Shutterstock.com, 30; ©Mediscan/Alamy Stock Photo, 31

Graphic Element Credits: ©tukkki/Shutterstock.com, back cover, front cover, multiple interior pages; ©paprika/Shutterstock.com, back cover, front cover, multiple interior pages; ©Silhouette Lover/Shutterstock Images, multiple interior pages

45th Parallel Press is an imprint of Cherry Lake Publishing.

Library of Congress Cataloging-in-Publication Data

Names: Loh-Hagan, Virginia, author.
Title: Top 10—horrors / by Virginia Loh-Hagan.
Other titles: Horrors
Description: Ann Arbor : Cherry Lake Press, 2016. | Includes bibliographical references and index.
Identifiers: LCCN 2015050713| ISBN 9781634710992 (hardcover) | ISBN 9781634711982 (pdf) |
    ISBN 9781634712972 (pbk.) | ISBN 9781634713962 (ebook)
Subjects: LCSH: Dangerous animals—Juvenile literature.
Classification: LCC QL100 .L648 2016 | DDC 591.6/5—dc23
LC record available at https://lccn.loc.gov/2015050713

Printed in the United States of America
Corporate Graphics

About the Author

Dr. Virginia Loh-Hagan is an author, university professor, former classroom teacher, and curriculum designer. She loves scary movies and scary stories. She lives in San Diego with her very tall husband and very naughty dogs. To learn more about her, visit: www.virginialoh.com.

TABLE OF CONTENTS

INTRODUCTION

Animals creep. They crawl. They make scary noises. They do scary things. They look scary. They inspire fear. Fear is a basic feeling. It doesn't let us do dangerous things. It warns us. It tells us to be careful.

Animals scare humans. Humans scream. They hide. They attack. They fear the unknown.

Animals are scared of humans, too. Humans have weapons. They're at the top of the food chain.

Some animals are extremely scary. They're scarier than other animals. The biggest scares happen in the animal world!

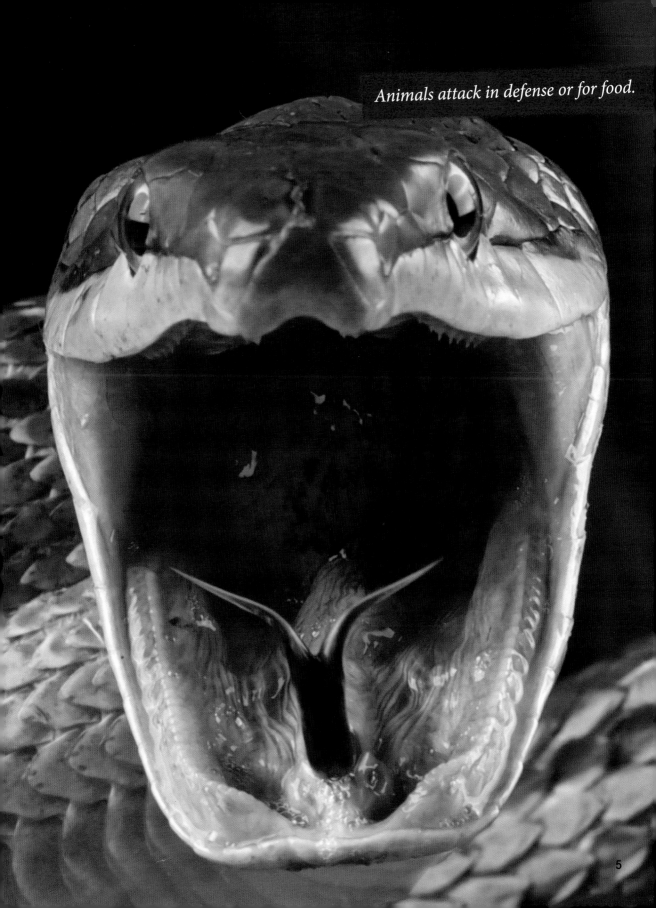

Chapter one

WOLVES

Wolves live in the northern part of the world. They're scary **predators**. Predators are hunters. Wolves attack animals fives times bigger than humans.

Wolves are known as man-eaters. Three types attack humans. First are wolves that have never seen humans. Second are wolves that have gotten too used to humans. Third are wolves that have **rabies**. Rabies is a bad sickness. But most wolves don't attack humans. They stay away from humans.

Wolves are the largest members of the dog family.

But humans are still scared of them. Many stories feature the big, bad wolf. Wolves have scary howls.

Wolf packs usually have 6 to 10 wolves.

Wolves eat anything to survive. Their perfect meal is large deer, moose, or elk. They kill as a **pack**. A pack is a group of wolves. They pick **prey**. Prey is an animal hunted for food. Wolves run it down. They gang up on it. They rip away legs. They rip at the guts. They wait for their prey to fall down. Then, they eat right away. They sometimes eat prey while the prey is still alive.

HUMANS DO WHAT?!?

What's scarier than a vampire? Maria Cristerna changed her body. She became "Vampire Lady." She inserted horns in her head. She's covered in tattoos. She made her teeth into fangs. People were scared of her. They avoided her. They crossed the street when she passed. They thought she was the devil. They thought she was on drugs. They thought she was crazy. She said, "I have always been very different. ... I am expressing beauty through my art for the world to see." She's from Mexico. She was a lawyer. She became a video jockey. She travels the world.

chapter two
MICE

Mice live everywhere. They live outside. They live inside.
They're small. They're harmless. They're scared of humans.
But humans are really scared of mice. A fear of mice is
common.

Mice get in and out of small spaces. They surprise people.
They move quickly. They're hard to catch.

Female mice can have up to 11 babies. They do this every
3 weeks. They're hard to control.

Mice can spread diseases.

South Australia had a huge mouse attack. Half a billion mice destroyed crops. They ate live farm animals. The attack lasted 6 months. It cost billions of dollars.

Chapter three

PIRANHAS

Piranhas are fish. They live in South America. They live in rivers. They have sharp teeth. They have powerful jaws. They have strong bites. They love eating meat.

A group of fish is a **school**. A school of piranhas hunt together. They could eat a cow in a few minutes. Luckily, they're **scavengers**. They usually eat dead animals. They eat tail fins. They eat fish scales. They don't usually eat whole animals.

Piranhas can tear meat.

Still, humans fear getting attacked. There's a reason for that.
A 6-year-old girl fell out of her grandmother's canoe.
Piranhas ate both her legs. She died.

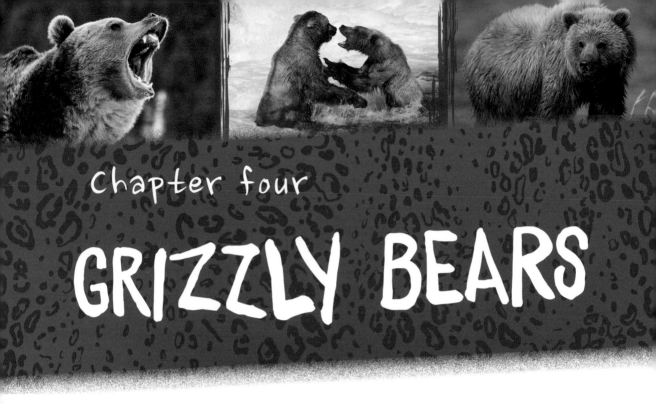

chapter four

GRIZZLY BEARS

Grizzly bears live in North America. They can grow to 8 feet tall (2.4 meters). They can weigh over 1,000 pounds (453.5 kilograms). They're huge. They have powerful jaws. They can crush bones. They're fast for their size. They can run 30 miles (48 kilometers) an hour. Humans are scared of their size and strength.

They're **omnivores**. They eat meat. But they mainly eat nuts, fruits, berries, leaves, and roots. Their poop helps nature. It spreads seeds around.

One swipe of a grizzly bear's paw is deadly.

They can be dangerous to humans. They attack when surprised. They attack when humans come between a mother and her **cubs**. Cubs are babies.

Chapter five

GREAT WHITE SHARKS

Great white sharks live in the ocean. They live around Australia, South Africa, California, and the northeastern United States. They're the largest predatory fish. They grow to 20 feet (6 m). They weigh 4,000 pounds (1,814.4 kg). They have 2 tons of muscles.

They have strong jaws. They have sharp teeth. They have 200 teeth at a time. They have five rows of teeth. Their teeth can get stuck in whatever they bite. They lose and replace teeth.

They're great hunters. They find prey easily. They see well.

Great white sharks have white bellies.

They hear well. Tiny holes around their snouts help them smell well. They feel movements. They're fast.

Great white shark babies swallow their own teeth while in the womb.

Great white sharks are scary. But they're scarier in people's minds. Falling coconuts kill more people than great white sharks. Humans taste bad to them. They have a hard time eating human bones.

They have **dorsal** fins. Dorsal means back. Seeing shark fins causes panic. Humans can't swim as well as sharks. They can't breathe underwater. The ocean is deep. It's open. Humans are scared of being trapped.

Great white sharks go for weeks without killing. They eat injured and sick animals. Without them, there'd be too many animals. They keep the oceans balanced.

DID YOU KNOW...?

- Large animals are used to being in charge. They dominate. But many still fear humans.

- People have phobias. Phobias are extreme fears. People get anxiety. Anxiety is high stress.

- Mice have great balance. They can walk across thin pieces of rope. They can climb walls.

- Baby bears have sharp claws. Adult bears have large claws. But their claws aren't as sharp. They wear down their claws.

- An adult king cobra's venom can kill an elephant. It can do it in a single bite.

- Vampire bats are the only mammals that live on blood alone. They need to drink about 1 ounce (28 grams) of blood at every meal.

Chapter six

VAMPiRE BATS

Vampire bats live in Central and South America. They hunt at night. They find sleeping victims. They find a warm spot on the skin. They use their teeth. They shave away hairs or fur. They make a small cut. They suck at the cut. Their tongue has a groove. It laps up blood.

Their spit is special. It makes their victims bleed. It **numbs** their prey. Numb means not feeling anything.

Some humans believe vampire bats are evil. Vampire bats eat blood. They fly. They live in caves. They live

Vampire bats suck blood without waking their prey.

underground. They live in dark buildings. They're mysterious.

Chapter seven

SPIDERS

Spiders live almost everywhere. They're predators. They hunt bugs. Some have fangs. Some have hairy legs. Some have **venom**. Venom is injected poison.

They trap their prey. They use silk to make webs. Their webs are strong. They can hold 4,000 times their weight. Prey fly into webs. They get stuck. Then, spiders wrap them up. They eat them.

Some humans have an extreme fear of spiders. They avoid spiders. They tape windows. They wear panty hose when

There are over 35,000 different kinds of spiders.

sleeping. They get panic attacks. Spiders do more help
than harm. They keep insects away.

chapter eight
BEES

Bees live almost everywhere. They can't live in extreme cold. Some bees have stingers. The stingers have venom. Bees attack as **swarms**. A swarm is a bunch of angry bees. Swarms are deadly. The bees attack together. They can take down predators.

Bees sting. Venom attacks nerves. It causes a burst of pain. It bothers skin. It can harm body parts. It hurts organs. It shocks bodies. It can cause death. Some humans are **allergic**. An allergy is a bad reaction. One in 1,000 humans is allergic to bee stings. A human can take 10 bee stings per pound. Five hundred stings could kill a child.

Bees pollinate, or help grow, plants. Some make honey.

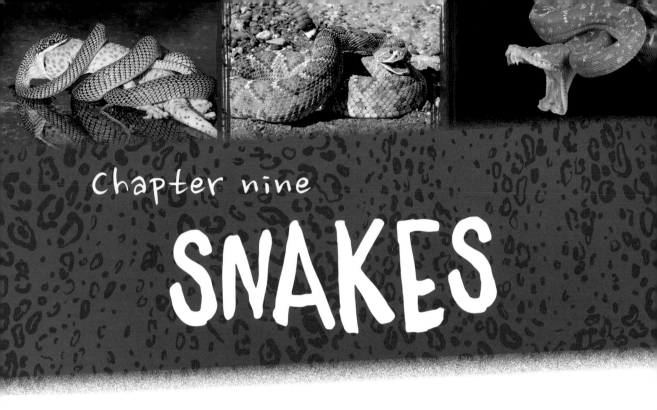

Chapter nine
SNAKES

Snakes live almost everywhere. Most snakes live in tropical areas.

They're great hunters. They track down prey. They hunt at night. They hunt during the day.

They have very strong senses. They have pits on the sides of their faces. These pits see special light. (Humans can't see this light. They can only feel its heat.) These pits send information to the brain. Snakes see the heat of their prey.

Each year around the world, snakes kill about 30,000 people.

This means nothing can hide. Snakes can see and feel prey. Luckily, snakes don't kill often. It takes them awhile to swallow. It takes them awhile to **digest**. Digest is how bodies break down food.

Snakes still bite after they die.

Most snakes have teeth. Some snakes have fangs. Snakes have a strong bite **reflex**. It's an instant movement. They just bite once. They bite quickly. Then, they move away. Their bites take less than a second.

They're **cold-blooded**. This means their body temperature changes with the environment. They don't have legs. They're low to the ground. They're sneaky. They don't blink. They have forked tongues.

Many humans fear snakes. They can be deadly. Less than 10 percent of snakes are poisonous. But most humans can't tell the difference. That's why they're scared.

WHEN ANIMALS ATTACK!

Alligators are scary. They have many sharp teeth. They have powerful jaws. They have scaly skin. James Morrow was in Florida. He went snorkeling. He was swimming underwater. He was attacked. An alligator bit his throat. It bit his neck. His head was in the alligator's mouth. He said, "I think my head was so far down his mouth that I touched his taste buds." Morrow is one of the few people to survive an alligator attack. The alligator cut his lung. It gave him several head injuries. Luckily, he was wearing a mask. The mask saved his life.

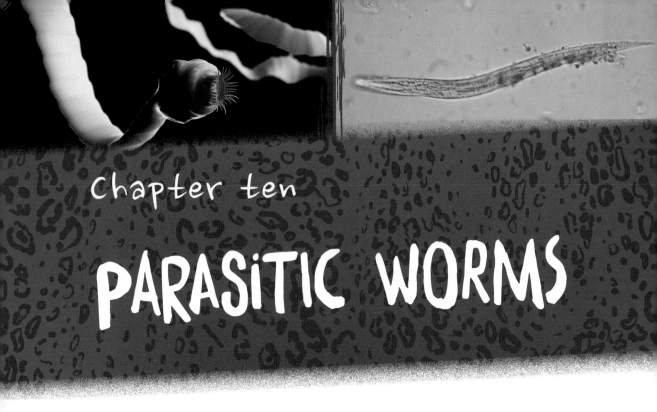

Chapter ten

PARASITIC WORMS

The scariest animals live inside bodies. Parasitic worms are man-eating monsters. **Parasites** live on a host. They depend on other animals for their lives. They live inside bodies. They attack guts. They attack blood. They attack hearts. They lay eggs near body organs. They grow. They eat. They destroy.

They can be 12 feet (3.6 m) long. They can live in bodies for several years. They cause sickness. They cause death. Most humans don't have parasitic worms living inside them. But most of those who do don't know it.

Humans can take medicines to help get rid of parasitic worms.

There's nowhere worms can't reach. They attack humans and animals. There's no hiding from worms. Worms are everywhere.

CONSIDER THIS!

TAKE A POSITION! Sometimes it's good to have fear. Fear keeps us safe. It makes us be careful. Should we fear animals? Is fear good or bad? Argue your point with reasons and evidence.

SAY WHAT? Even though humans are scared of animals, humans need them. Animals are important. Explain how animals help nature. Explain how they help humans.

THINK ABOUT IT! Animals tend to not eat humans. They're curious about humans. Some will give an exploratory bite. This means they bite to find out more. Most animals only attack humans to defend themselves. Humans have killed more animals than vice versa. So, why are we so scared of animals?

LEARN MORE!
- Cusick, Dawn. *Animals That Make Me Say Ouch!* Watertown, MA: Charlesbridge, 2014.
- *Scary Creatures* series: Children's Press.

GLOSSARY

allergic (uh-LUR-jik) having a bad reaction

cold-blooded (kohld-BLUHD-id) animals that change temperature to match the environment

cubs (KUBZ) baby bears

digest (dye-JEST) to break down food

dorsal (DOR-suhl) back

numbs (NUMZ) makes it so you can't feel anything

omnivores (AHM-nuh-vorz) animals that eat both meat and plants

pack (PAK) group of wolves or dogs

parasites (PAR-uh-sites) organisms living on a host

predators (PRED-uh-turz) hunters

prey (PRAY) animals that are hunted for food

rabies (RAY-beez) a bad illness spread by some animals

reflex (REE-fleks) an instant movement or reaction

scavengers (SKAV-uhn-jurz) animals that eat dead animals

school (SKOOL) group of fish

swarms (SWORMZ) groups of angry bees

venom (VEN-uhm) poison injected under the skin

INDEX